Easy Piano

GOLDEN HOUR
KACEY MUSGRAVES

ISBN 978-1-70510-560-3

Hal•Leonard®

Visit Hal Leonard Online at
www.halleonard.com

Contact us:
Hal Leonard
7777 West Bluemound Road
Milwaukee, WI 53213
Email: info@halleonard.com

In Europe, contact:
Hal Leonard Europe Limited
42 Wigmore Street
Marylebone, London, W1U 2RN
Email: info@halleonardeurope.com

In Australia, contact:
Hal Leonard Australia Pty. Ltd.
4 Lentara Court
Cheltenham, Victoria, 3192 Australia
Email: info@halleonard.com.au

SLOW BURN

Words and Music by KACEY MUSGRAVES,
IAN FITCHUK and DANIEL TASHIAN

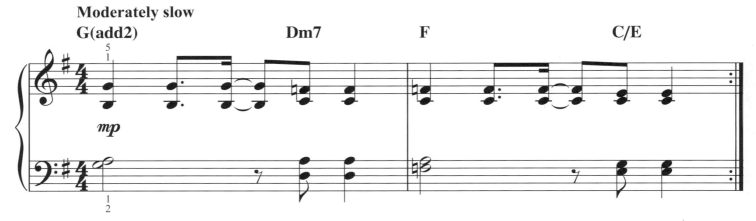

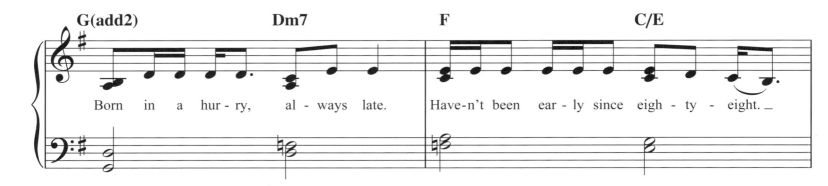

Born in a hur-ry, al-ways late. Have-n't been ear-ly since eigh-ty - eight.

Tex - as is hot, I can be cold.

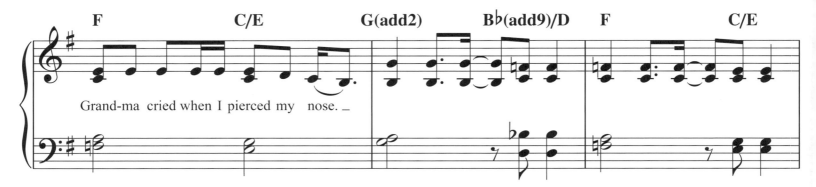

Grand-ma cried when I pierced my nose.

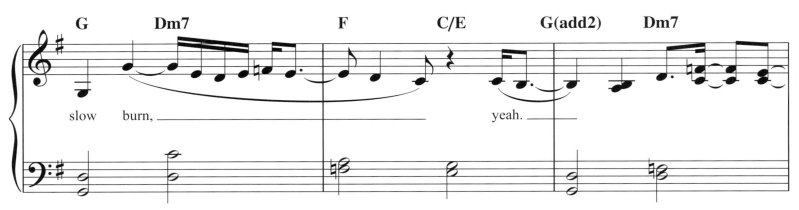

slow burn, _____ yeah.

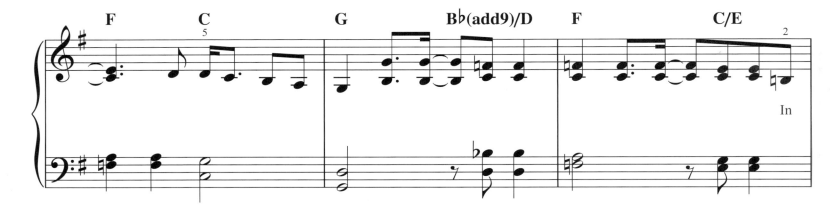

In

Ten - nes - see the sun's go - in' down but in Bei - jing they're head - in' out ___ to work.

You know the bar down the street don't close for an hour.

We should take a walk and look at all the flow - ers. ___

'Cause I'm al - right ___ with a slow burn. ___

Tak - in' my ___ time, ___ let the world turn. ___

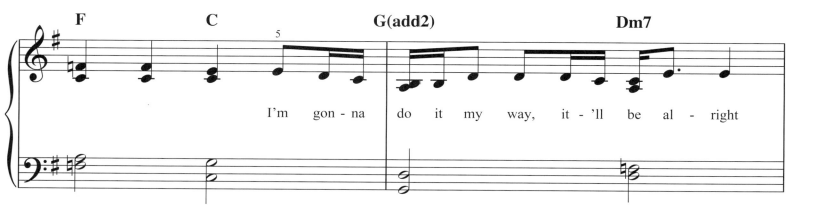

I'm gon - na do it my way, it -'ll be al - right

6

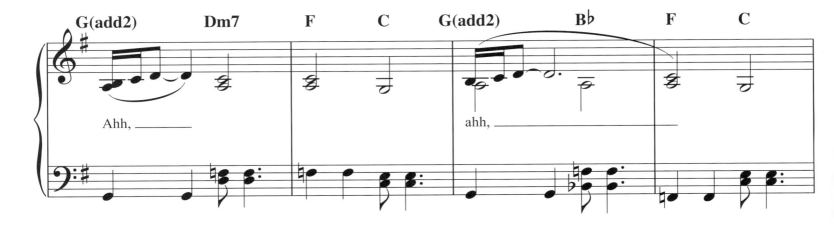

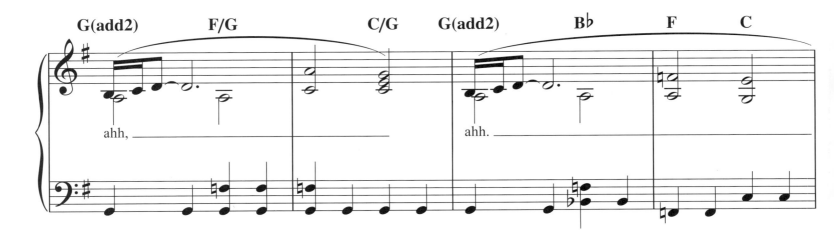

7

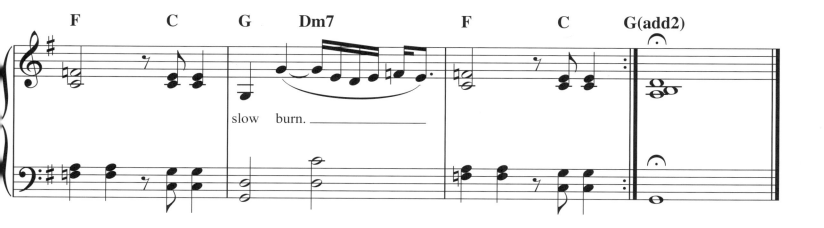

BUTTERFLIES

Words and Music by KACEY MUSGRAVES,
LUKE LAIRD and NATALIE HEMBY

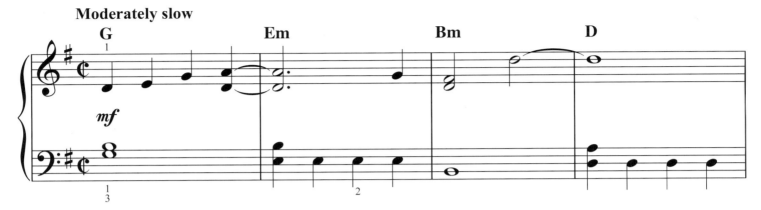

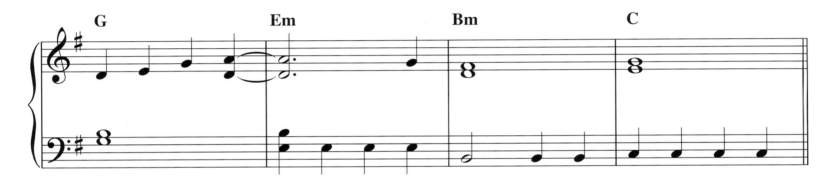

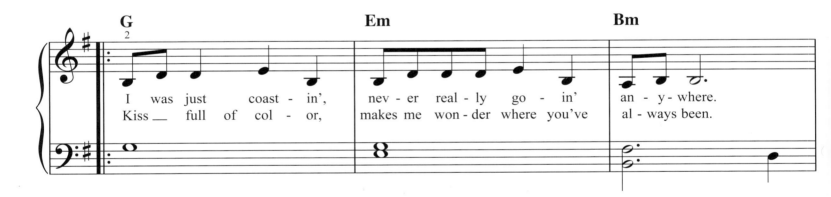

I was just coast - in', nev - er real - ly go - in' an - y - where.
Kiss ___ full of col - or, makes me won - der where you've al - ways been.

I was   Caught up in a web, I was   get - tin' kind - a used to
hid - in' in ___ doubt till you   brought ___ me ___ out of my

9

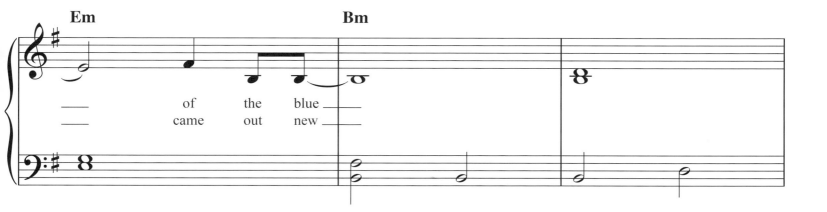

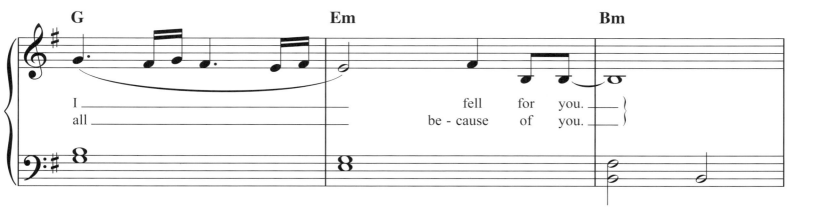

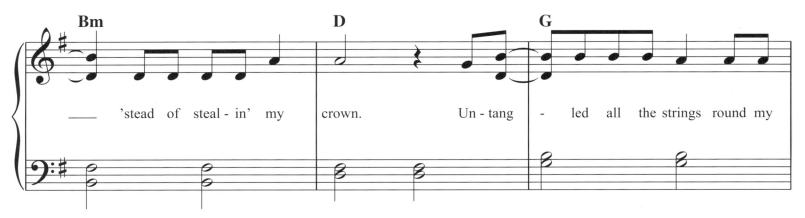

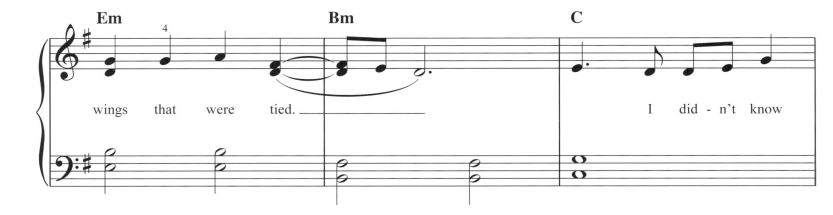

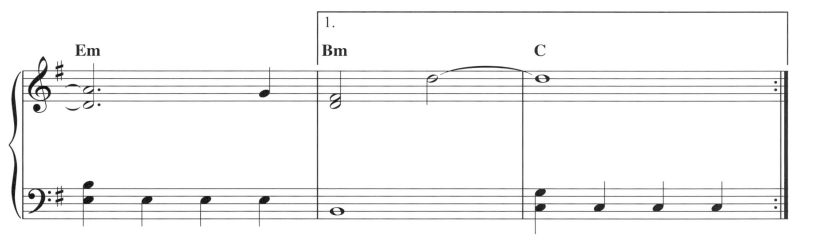

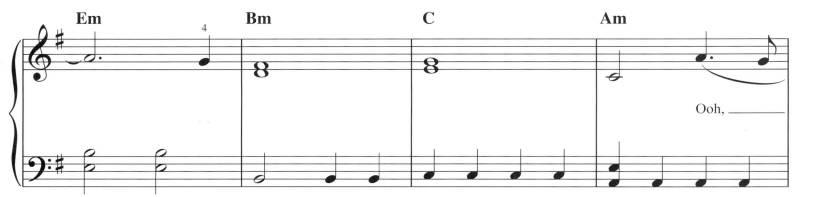

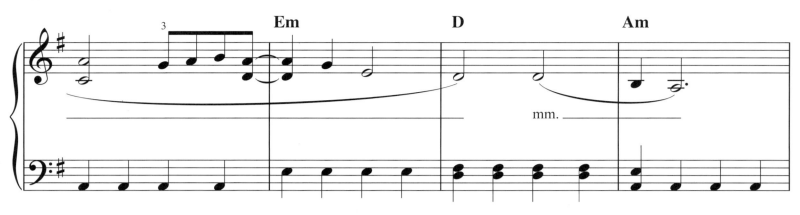

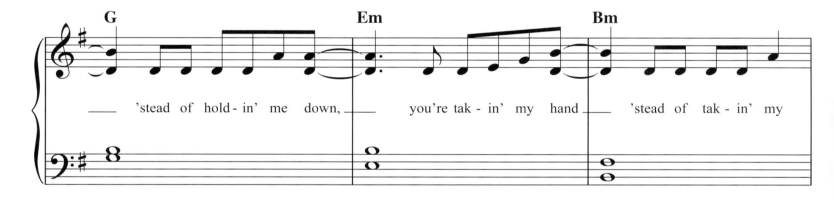

13

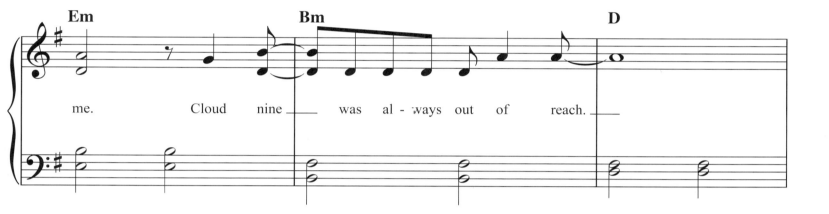

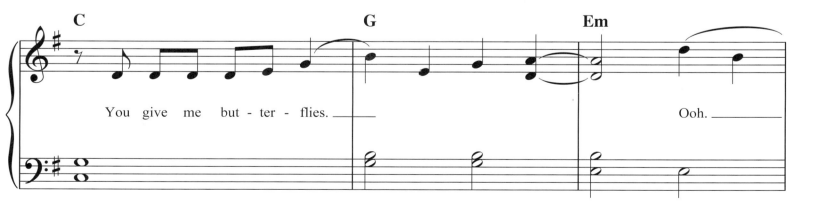

14

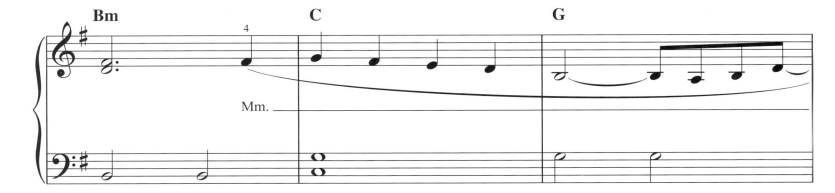

You gave me but-ter-flies.

Mm.

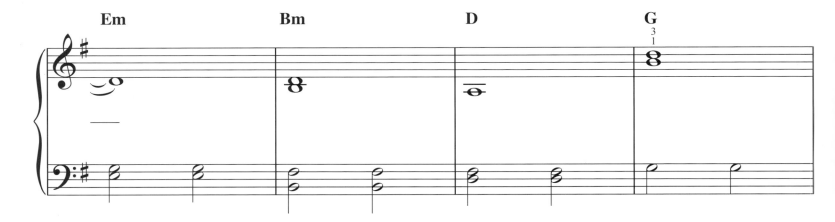

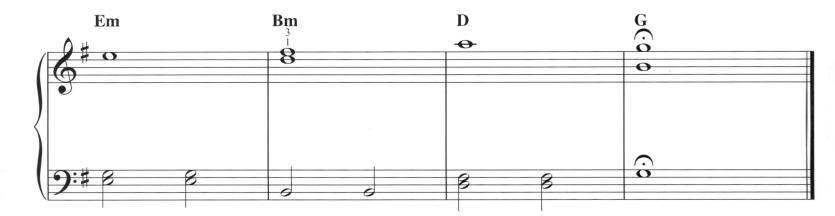

LONELY WEEKEND

Words and Music by KACEY MUSGRAVES,
IAN FITCHUK and DANIEL TASHIAN

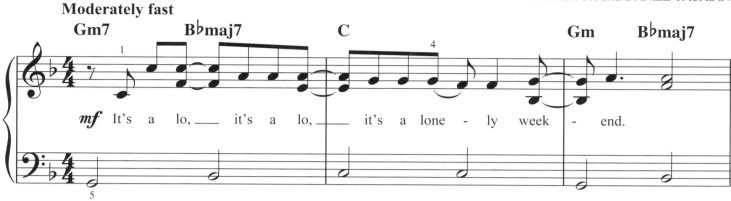

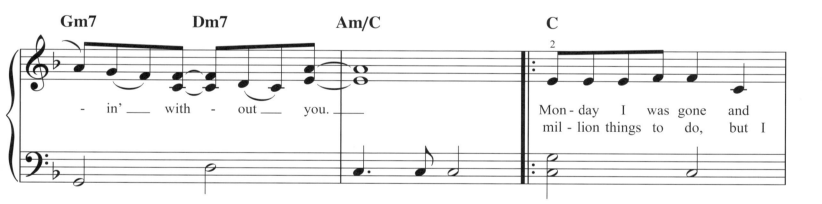

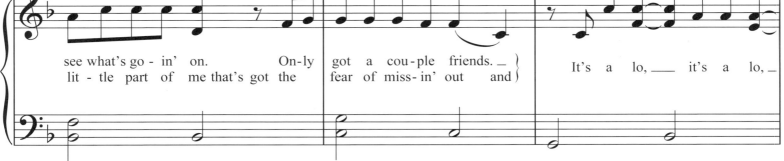

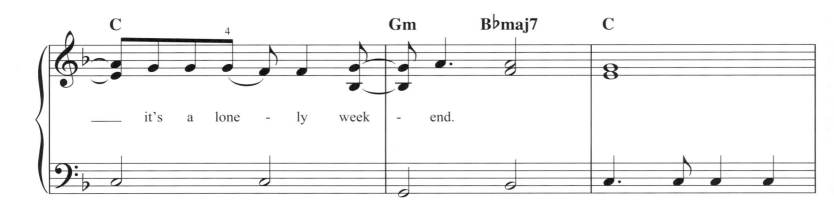

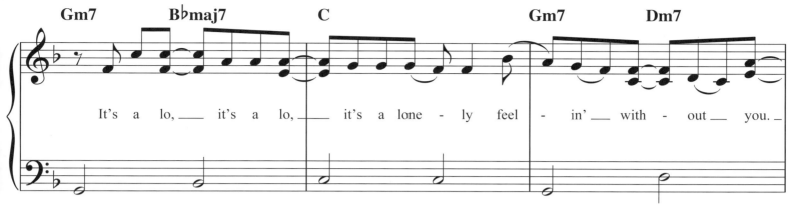

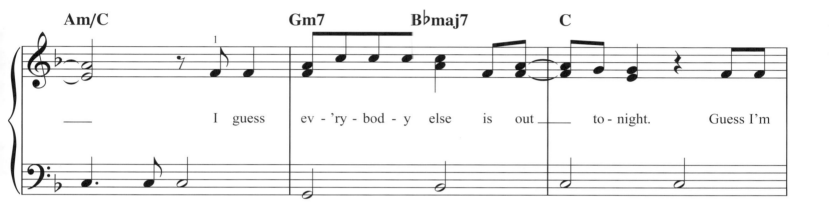

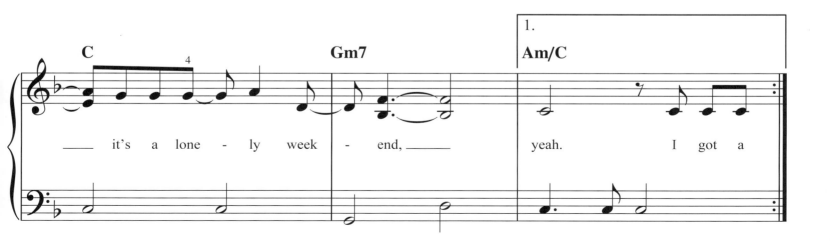

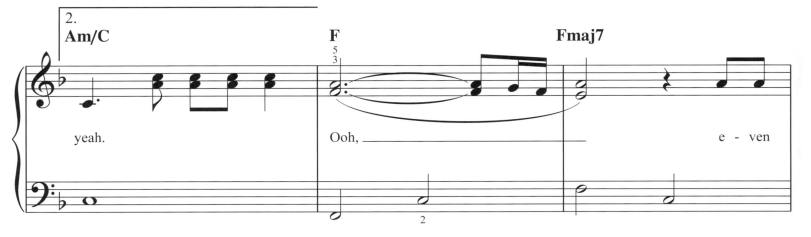

yeah. Ooh, _____ e - ven

if you got some-bod - y on ____ your __ mind, __ ooh, _____

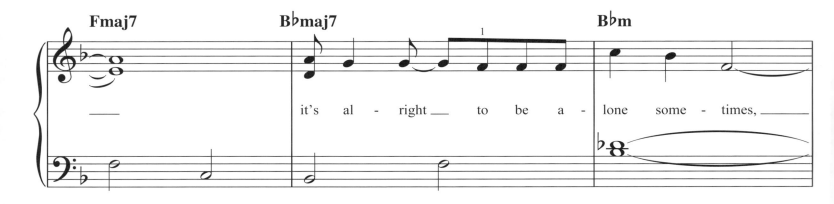

____ it's al - right ___ to be a - lone some - times, _____

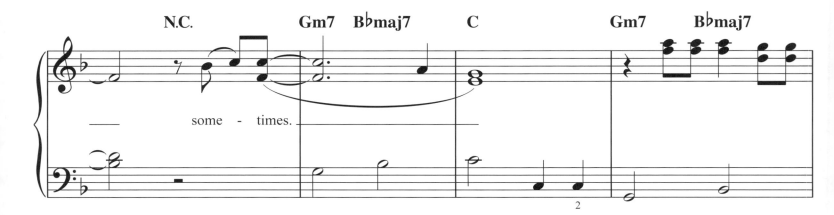

____ some - times. _____

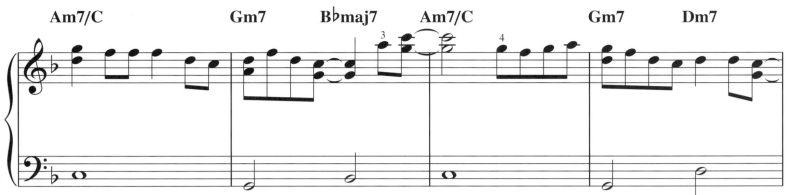

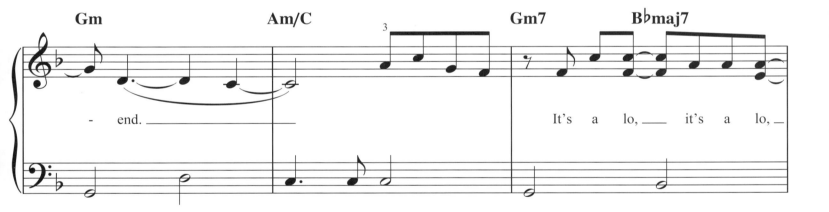

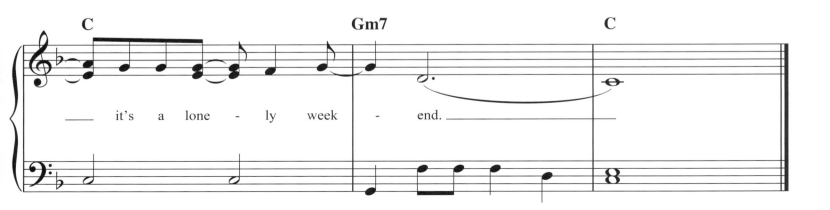

LOVE IS A WILD THING

Words and Music by KACEY MUSGRAVES,
IAN FITCHUK and DANIEL TASHIAN

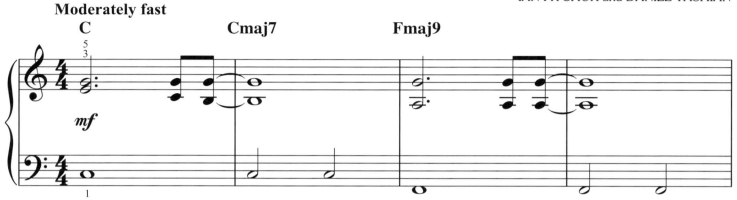

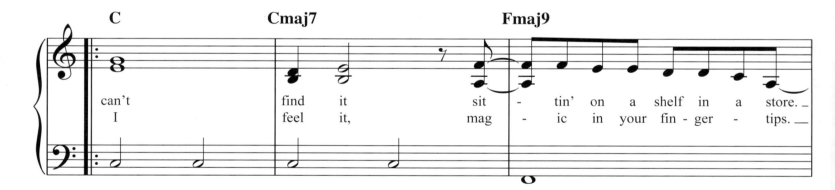

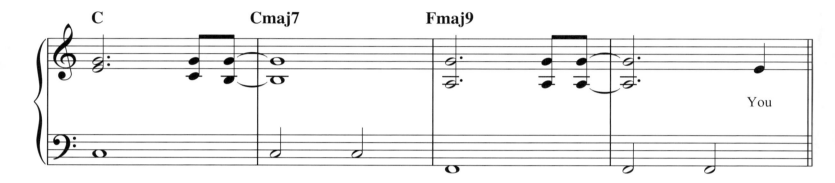

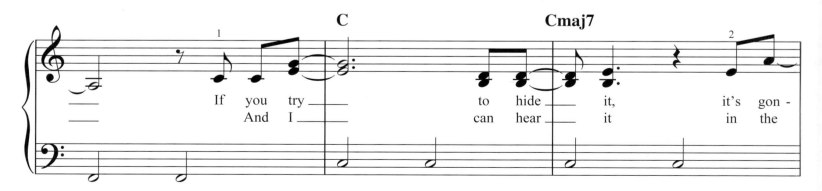

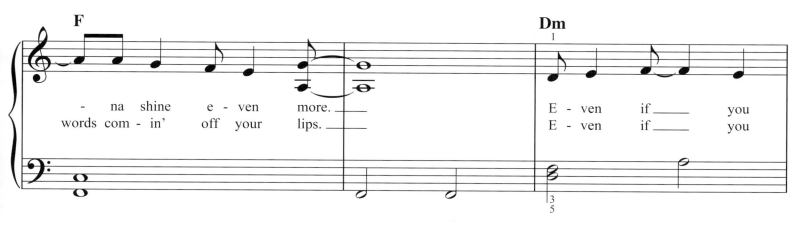
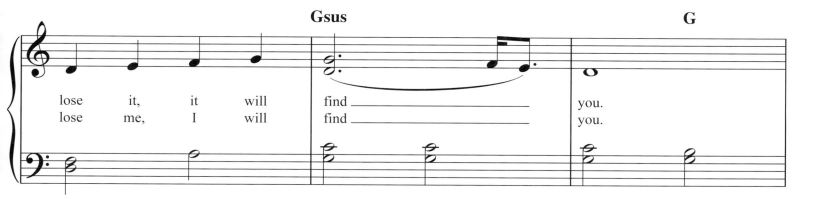

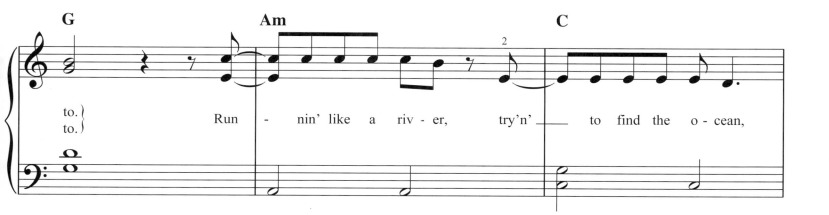

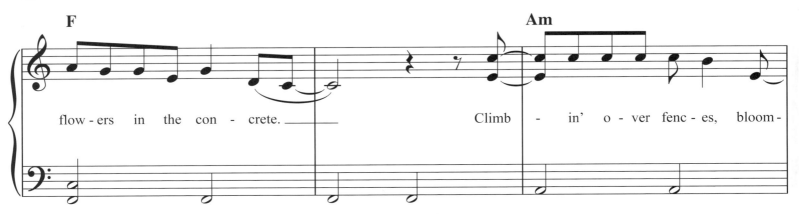

flow-ers in the con-crete. Climb - in' o - ver fenc-es, bloom-

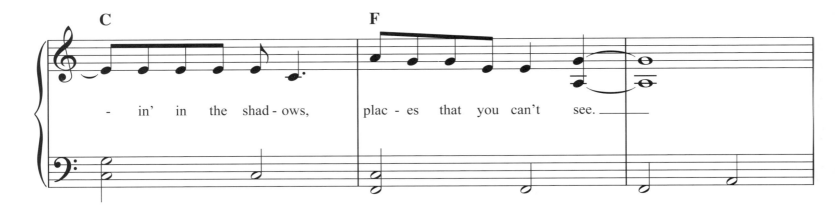

- in' in the shad-ows, plac-es that you can't see.

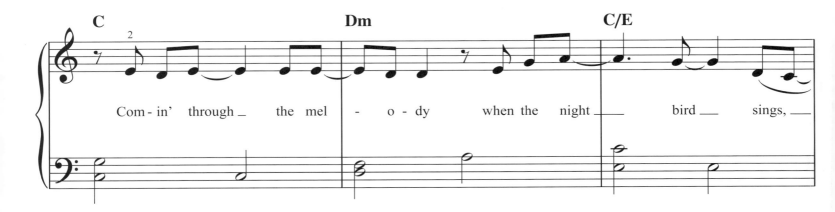

Com-in' through the mel - o-dy when the night bird sings,

love is a wild thing,

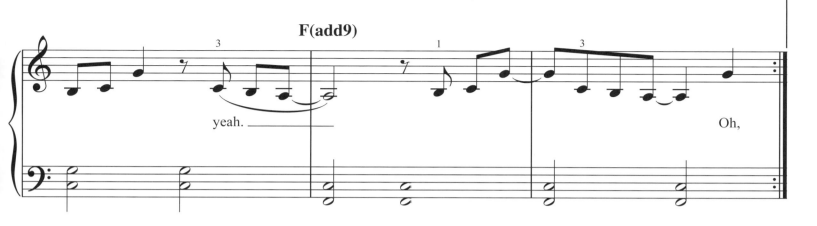

yeah. Oh,

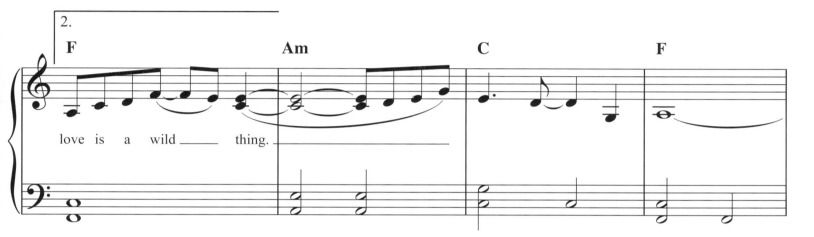

2.

love is a wild thing.

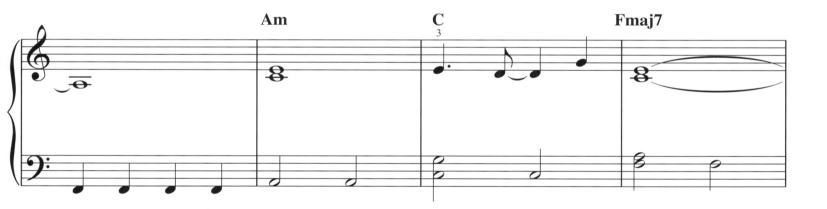

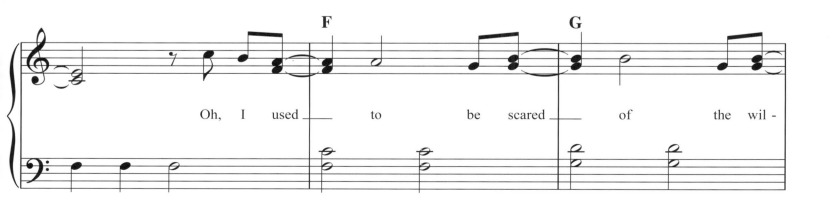

Oh, I used to be scared of the wil-

24

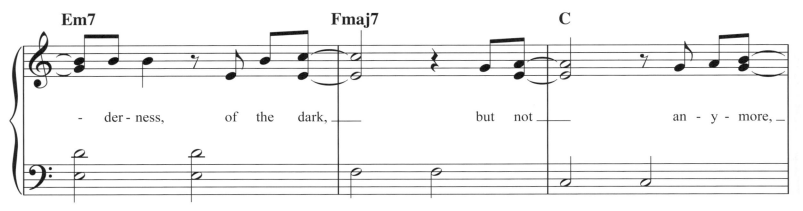

- der - ness, of the dark, but not an - y - more,

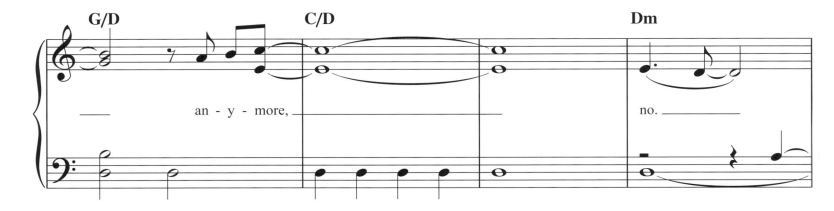

an - y - more, no.

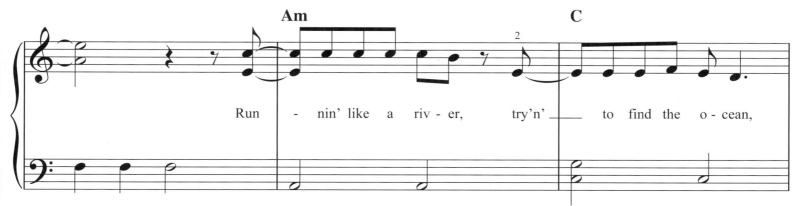

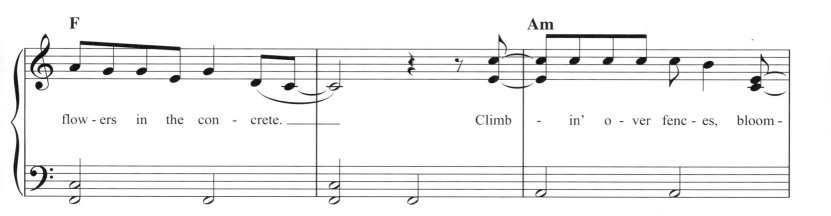

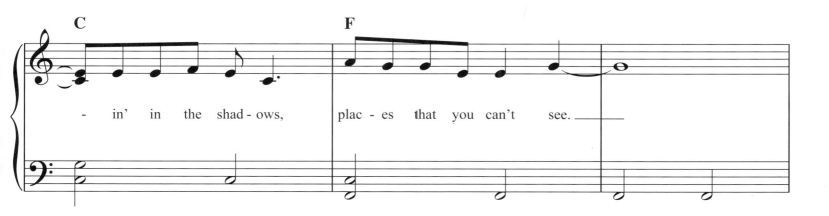

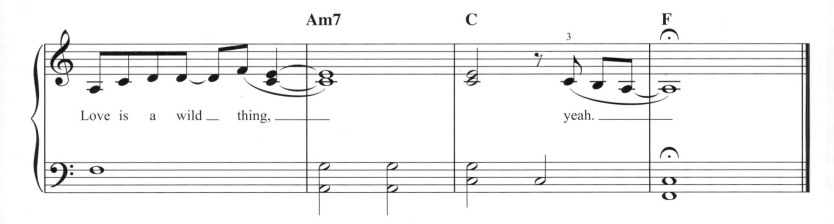

OH, WHAT A WORLD

Words and Music by KACEY MUSGRAVES,
IAN FITCHUK and DANIEL TASHIAN

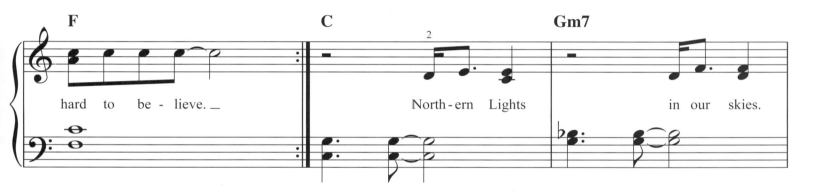

28

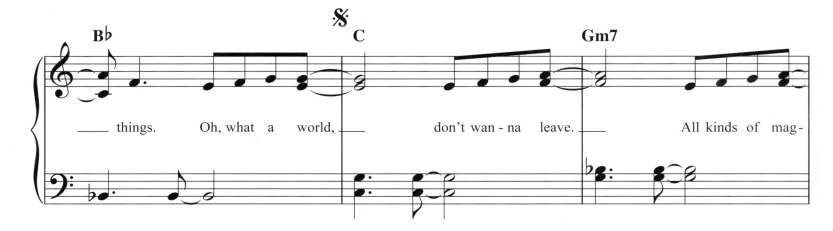

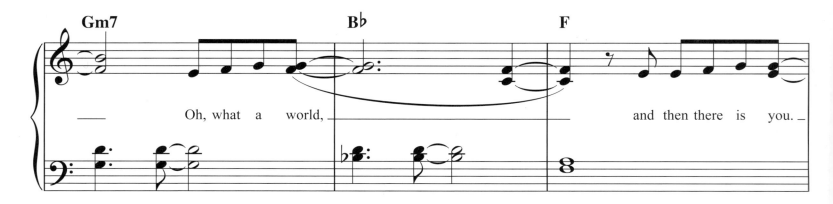

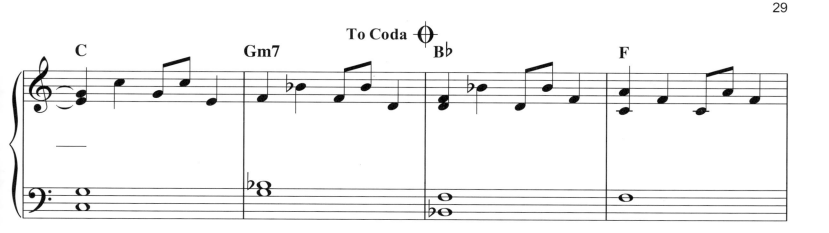

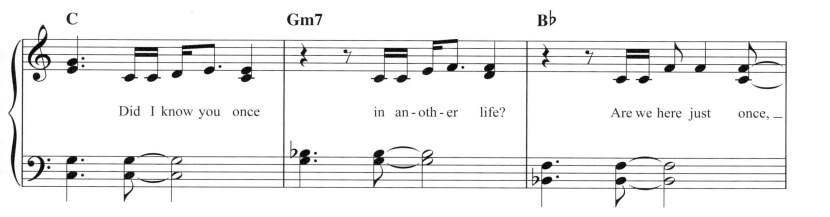

30

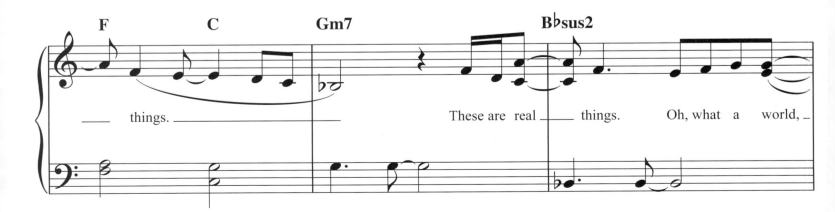

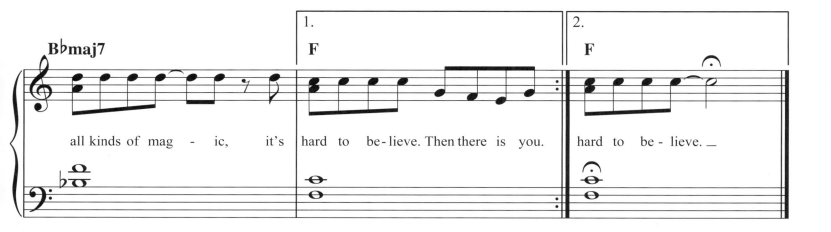

MOTHER

Words and Music by KACEY MUSGRAVES,
IAN FITCHUK and DANIEL TASHIAN

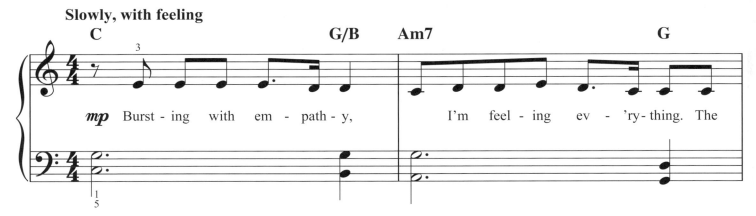

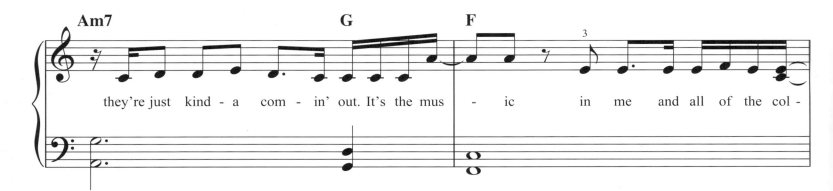

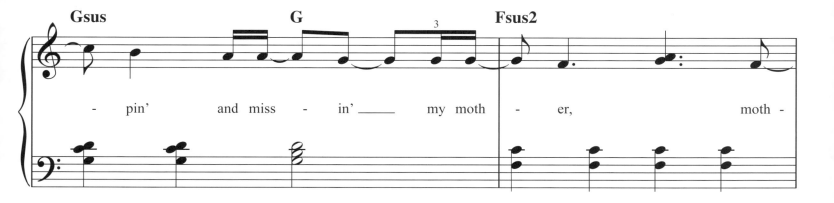

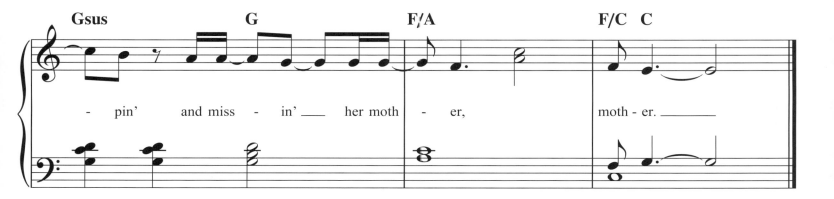

SPACE COWBOY

Words and Music by KACEY MUSGRAVES,
LUKE LAIRD and SHANE McANALLY

Moderate Ballad

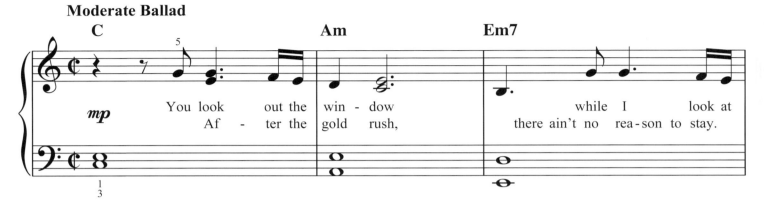

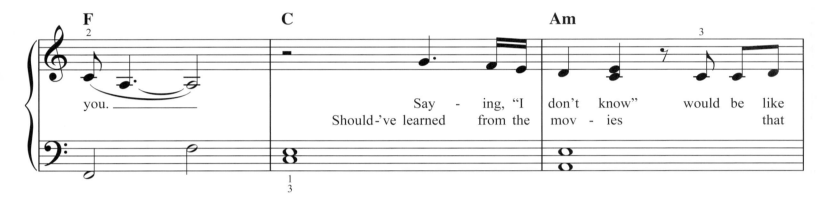

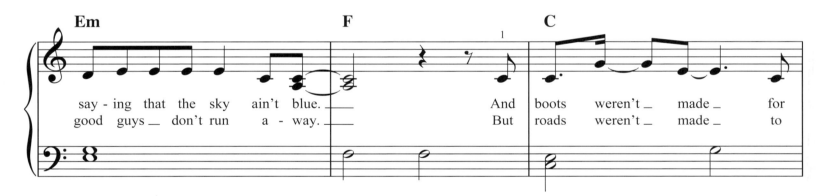

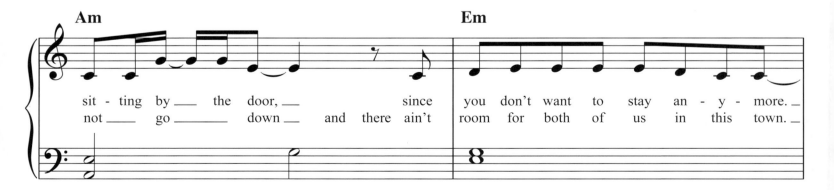

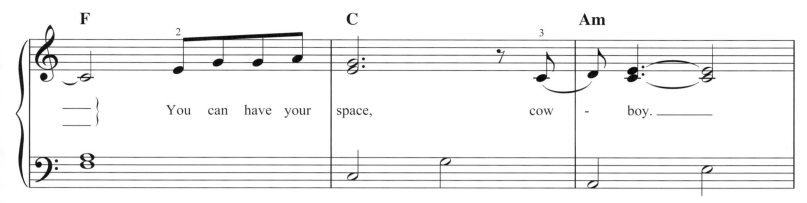

You can have your space, cow - boy.

I ain't gon - na fence you in. Go on, ride a - way in your Sil -

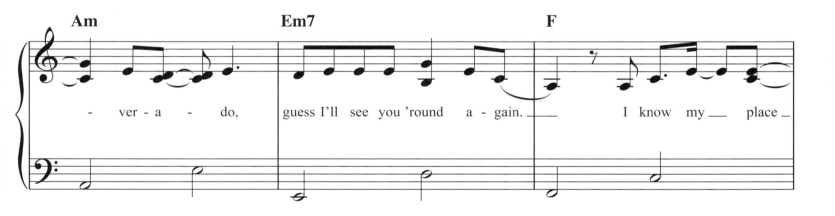

- ver - a - do, guess I'll see you 'round a - gain. I know my ___ place ___

___ and it ain't with ___ you, ___ well, sun - sets fade ___ and love does

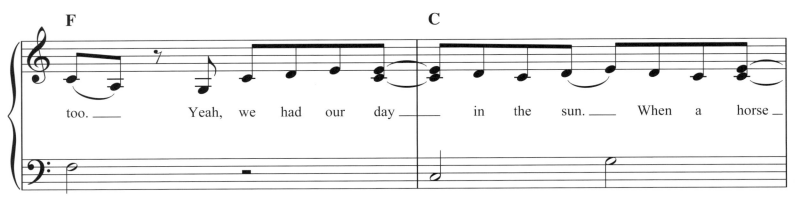

too. ____ Yeah, we had our day ____ in the sun. ____ When a horse ___

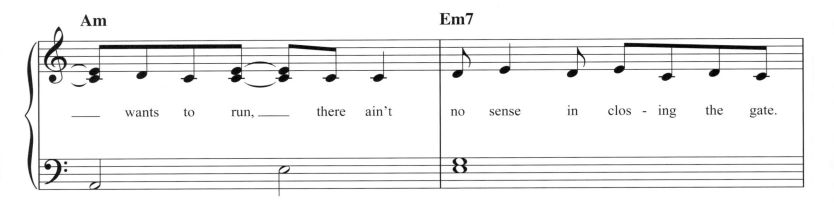

___ wants to run, ___ there ain't no sense in clos - ing the gate.

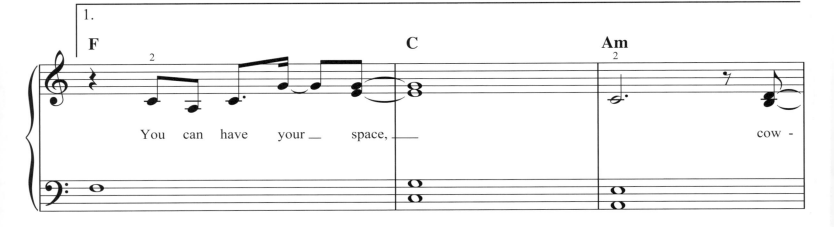

1.

You can have your _ space, ___ cow -

2.

- boy. ___ So you can have your _ space. _

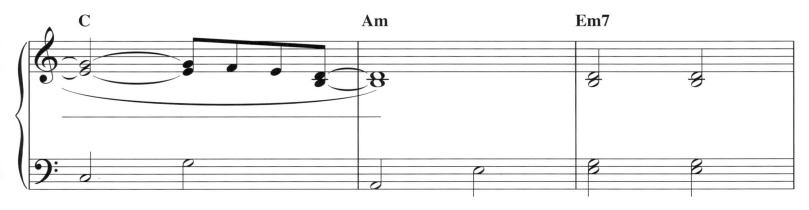

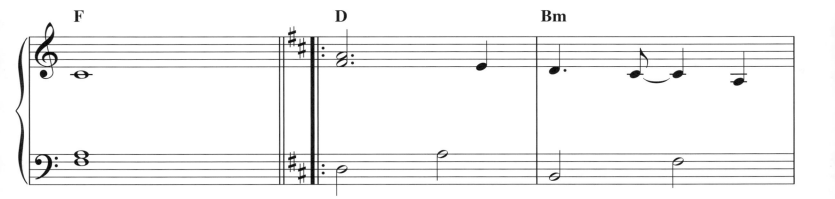

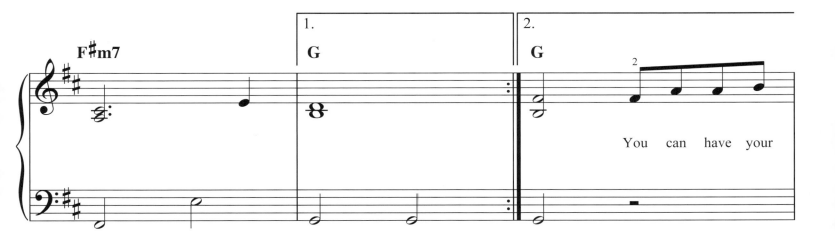

You can have your

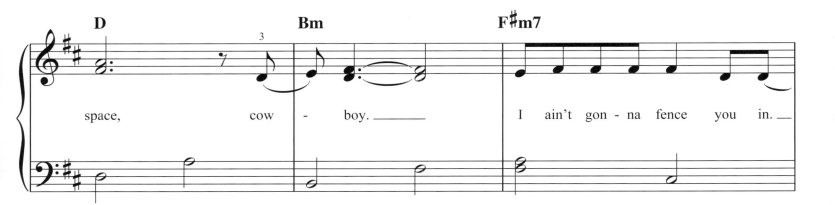

space, cow - boy. _____ I ain't gon - na fence you in. _____

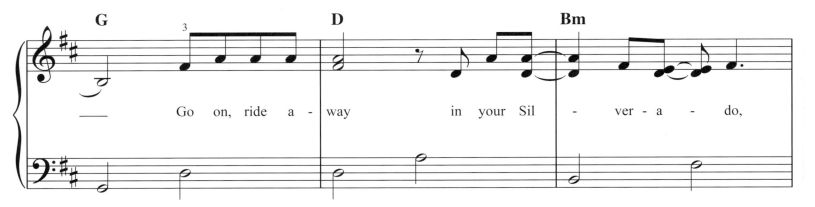

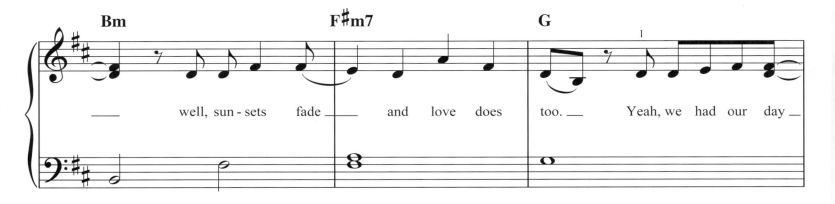

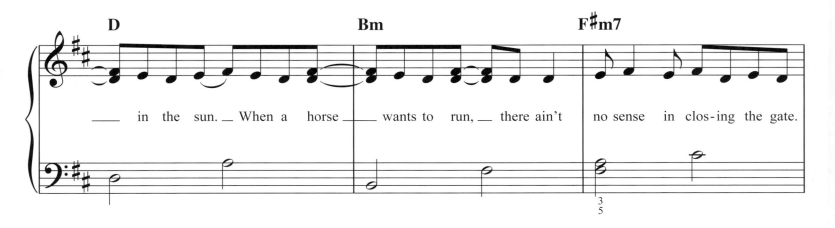

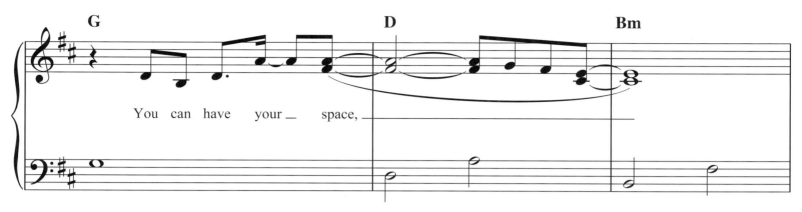

You can have your __ space,

yeah, __ you can have your __ space.

You can have your __ space, __

cow - boy. __

HAPPY & SAD

Words and Music by KACEY MUSGRAVES,
IAN FITCHUK and DANIEL TASHIAN

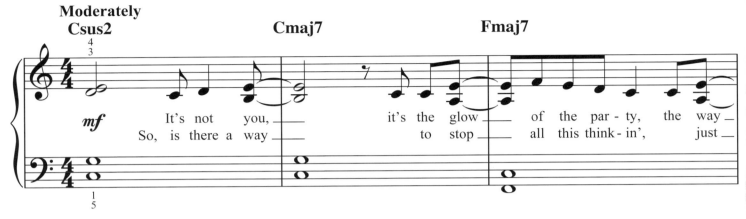

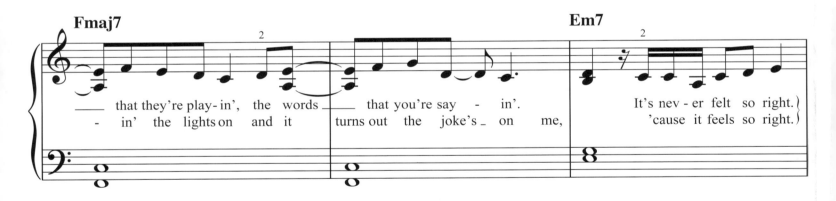

41

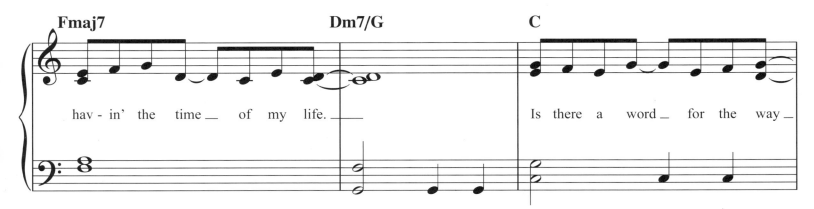

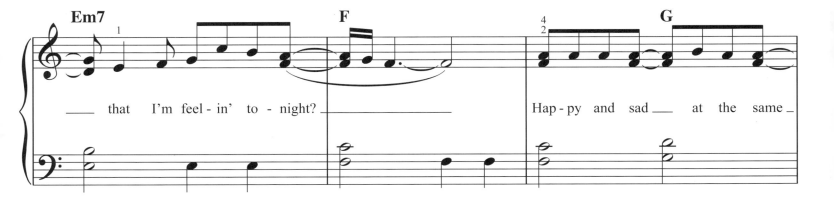

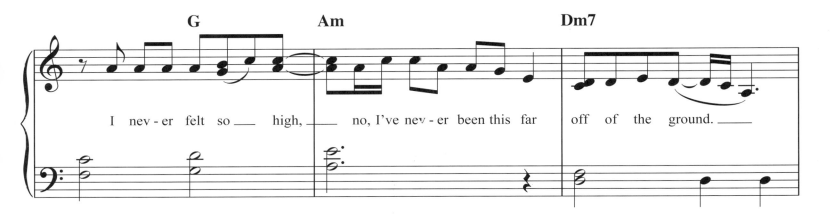

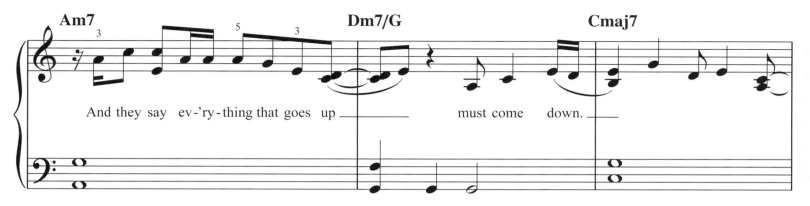

43

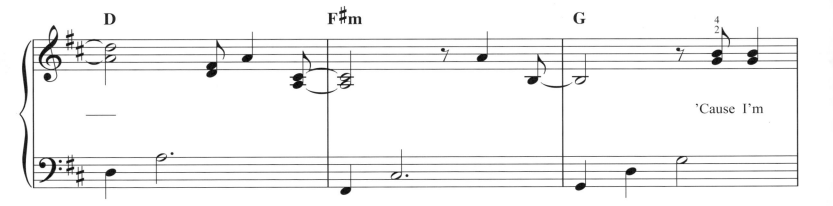

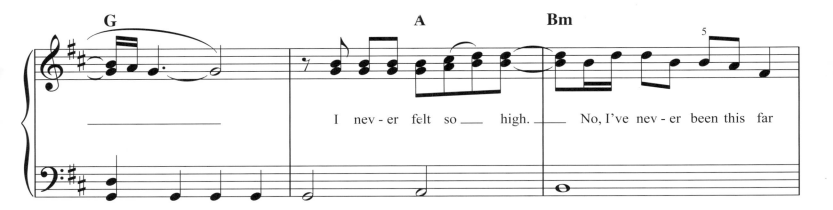

44

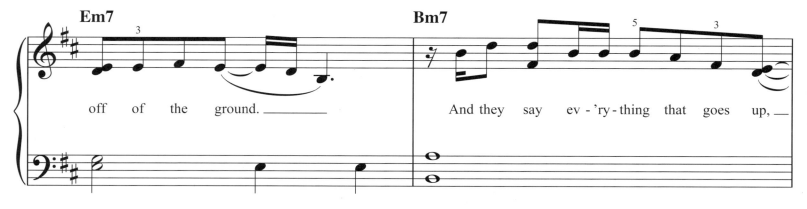

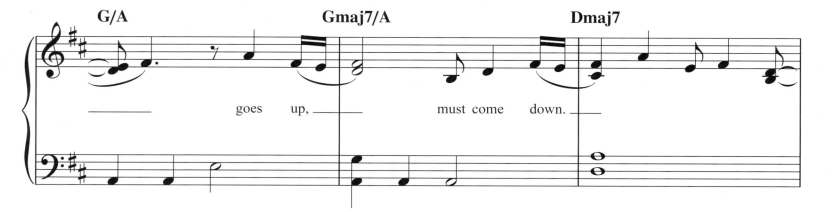

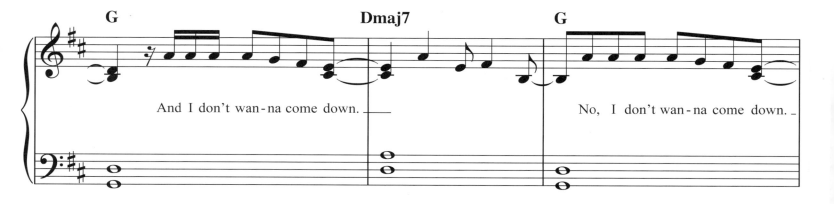

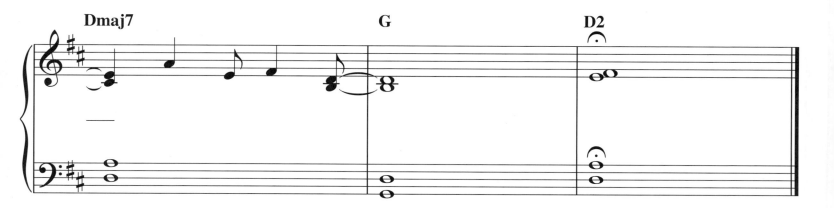

VELVET ELVIS

Words and Music by KACEY MUSGRAVES,
NATALIE HEMBY and LUKE DICK

Country Rock beat

All I ev-er want-ed was some-thing clas-sic, the kind of

love song that goes on 'til the end __ of time. __ All I ev-er want-ed was a lit-tle

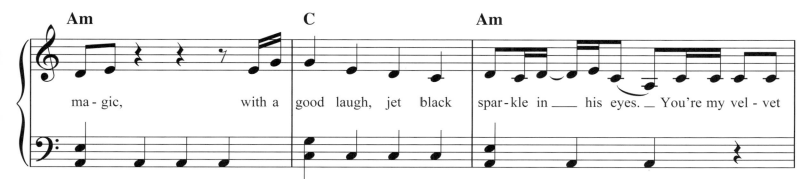

ma-gic, with a good laugh, jet black spar-kle in __ his eyes. __ You're my vel-vet

El - vis, I ain't nev - er gon - na take you down. Mak - ing ev - 'ry - bod - y

jeal - ous ___ when they step in - to my house. Soft to the touch, feels like love,

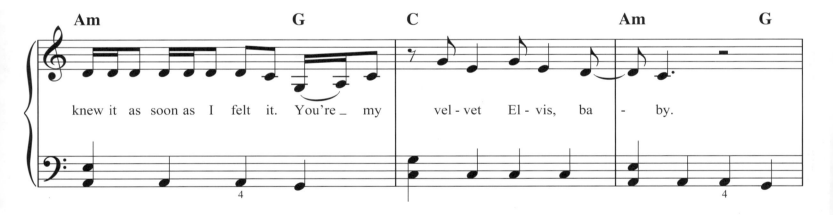

knew it as soon as I felt it. You're _ my vel - vet El - vis, ba - by.

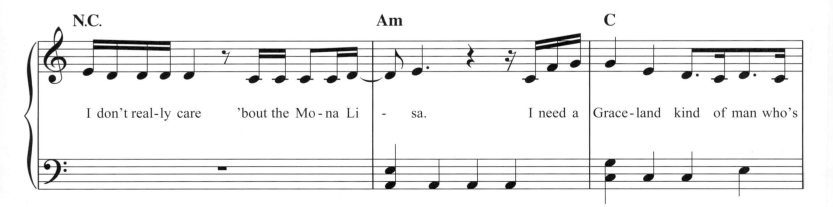

I don't real - ly care 'bout the Mo - na Li - sa. I need a Grace - land kind of man who's

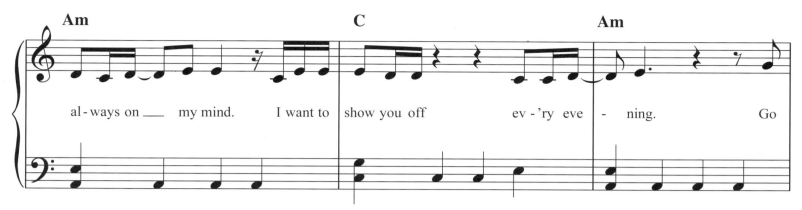

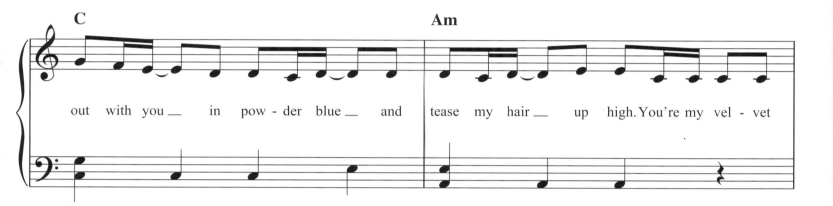

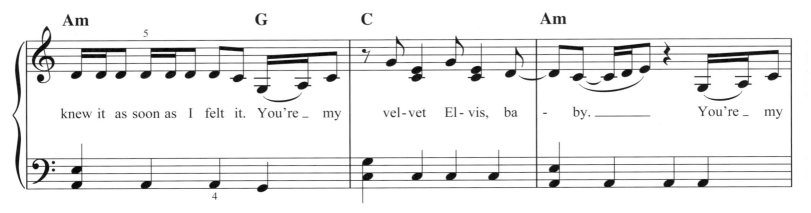

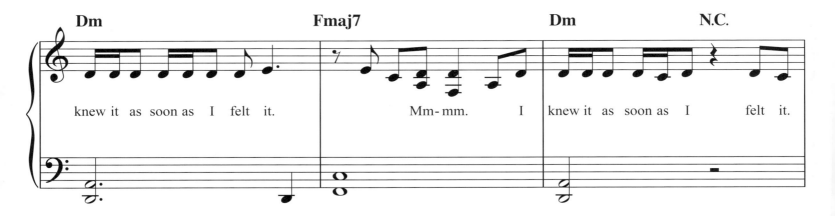

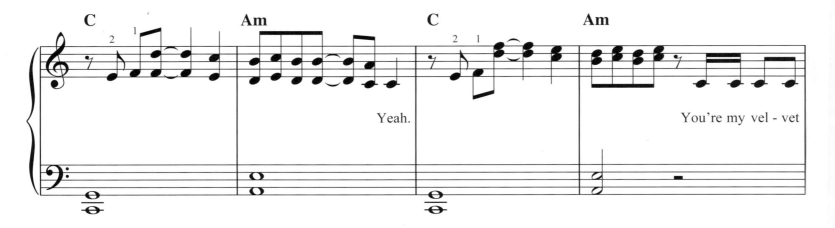

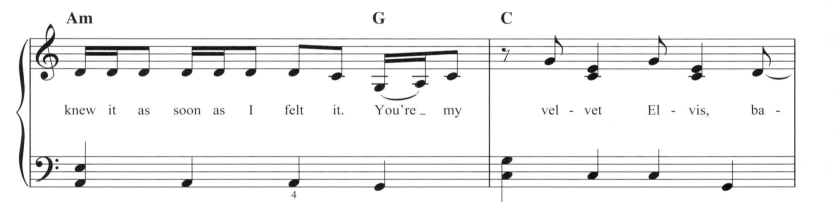

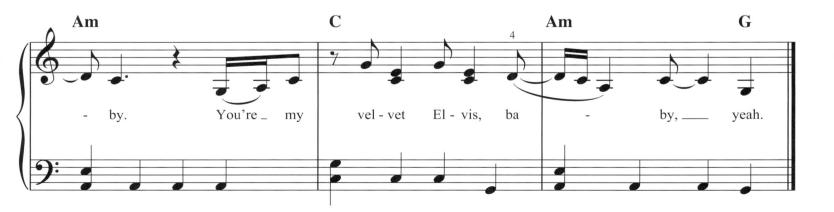

WONDER WOMAN

Words and Music by KACEY MUSGRAVES,
JESSE FRASURE, AMY WADGE
and HILLARY LINDSEY

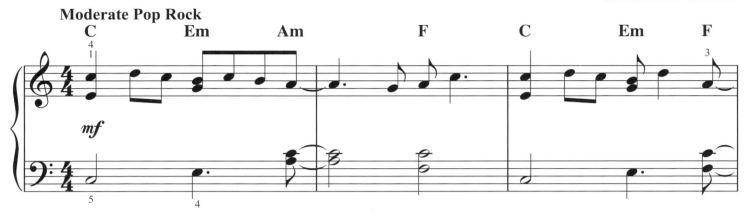

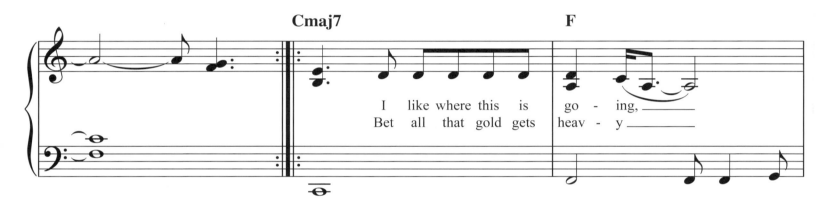

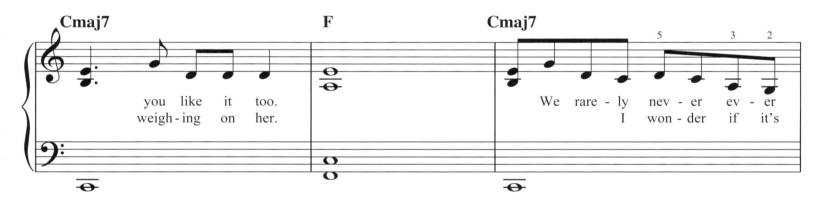

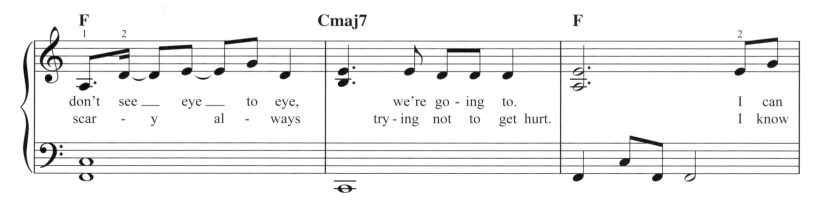

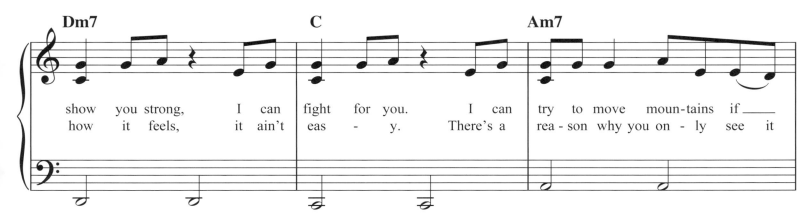

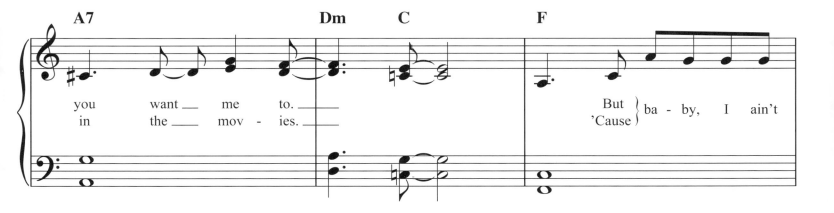

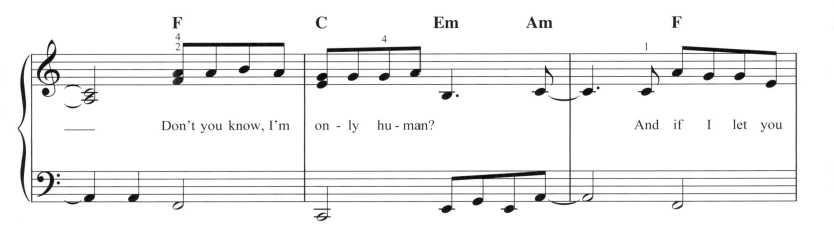

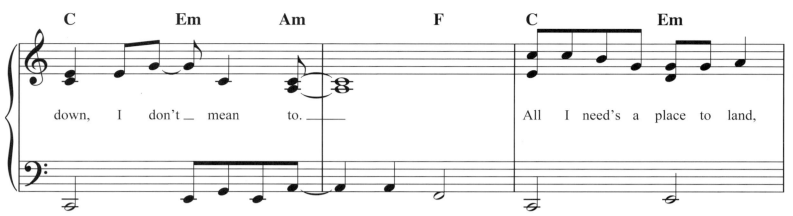

down, I don't __ mean to. __ All I need's a place to land,

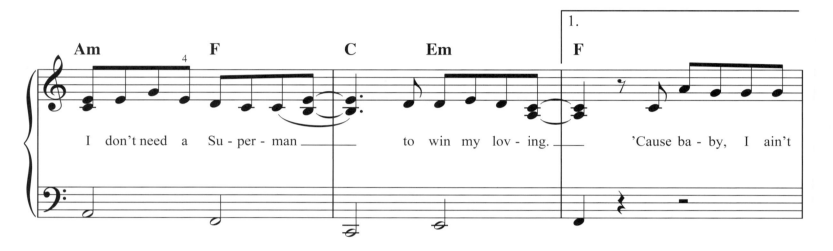

I don't need a Su-per-man __ to win my lov-ing. __ 'Cause ba-by, I ain't

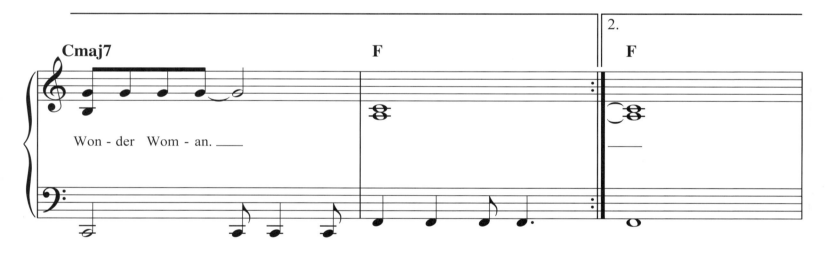

Won-der Wom-an. __

You don't know how __ to fly, __

no.　　Mmm.　　　　　That's o - kay,　　　nei - ther do I.

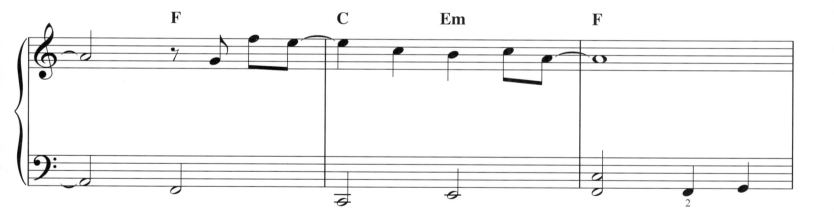

I know I ain't Won-der Wom-an. ____

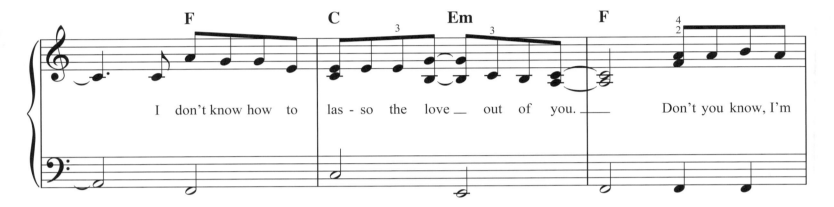

I don't know how to las-so the love __ out of you. ____ Don't you know, I'm

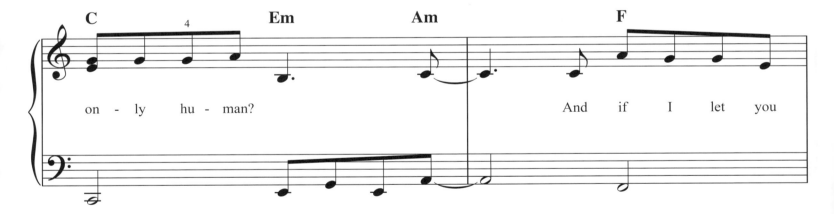

on - ly hu - man? And if I let you

down, I don't __ mean to. ____ All I need's a place to land,

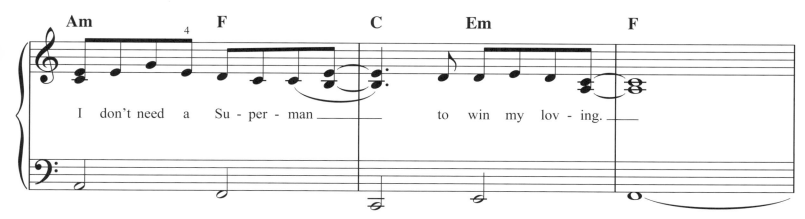

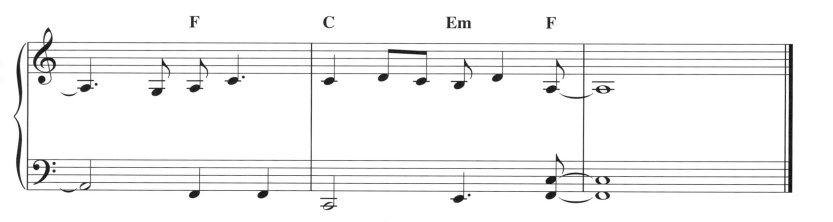

GOLDEN HOUR

Words and Music by KACEY MUSGRAVES,
IAN FITCHUK and DANIEL TASHIAN

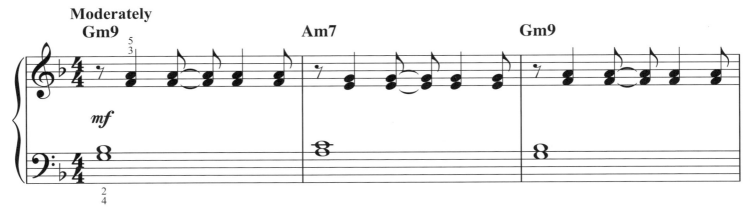

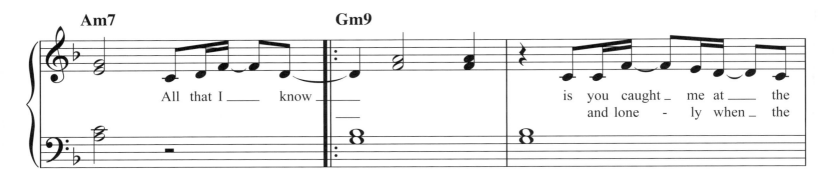

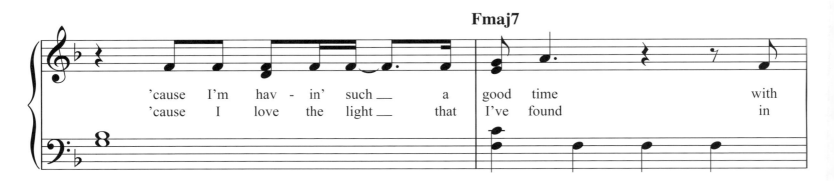

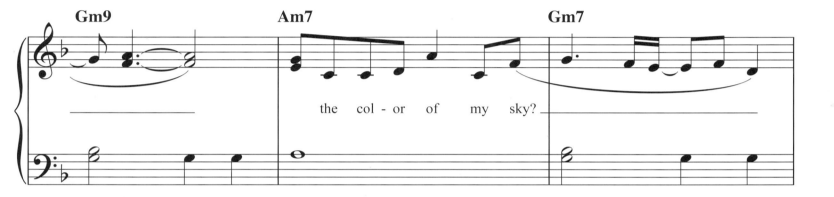

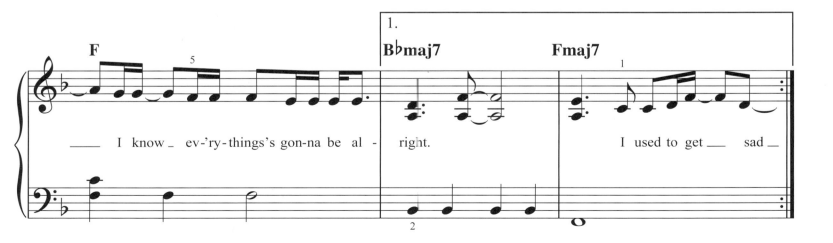

58

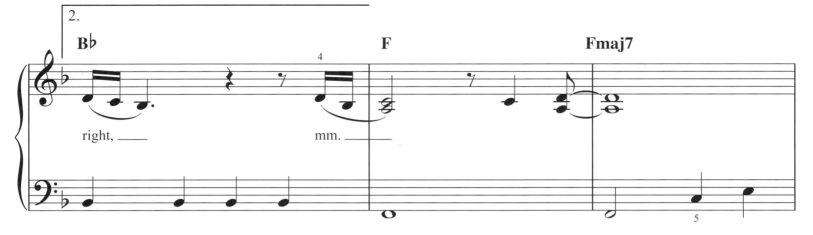

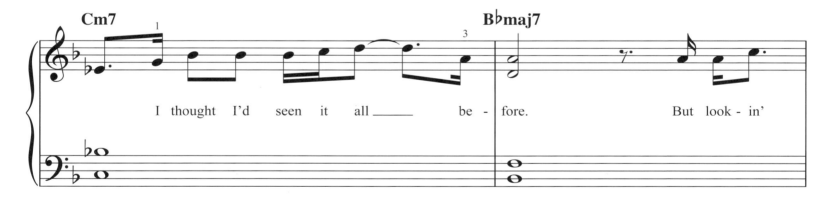

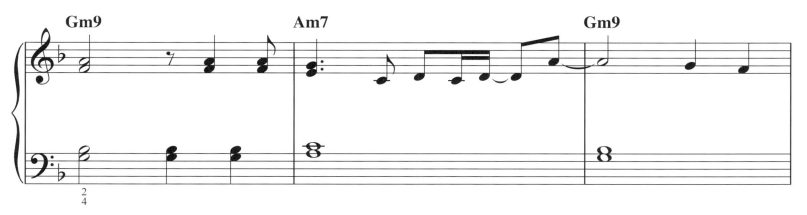

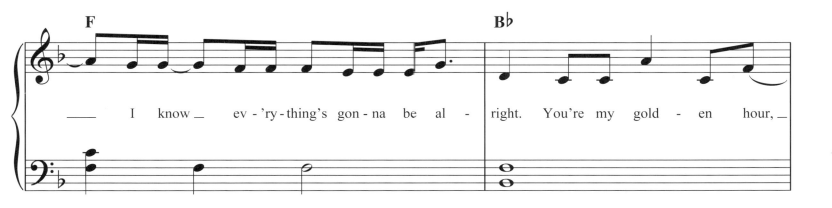

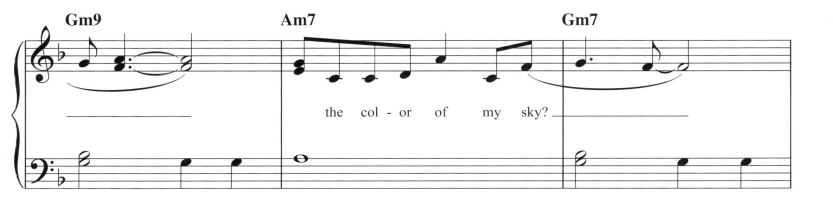

60

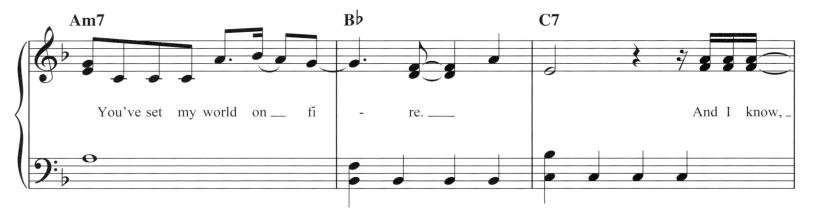

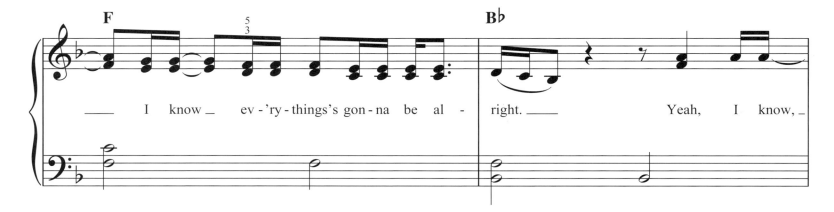

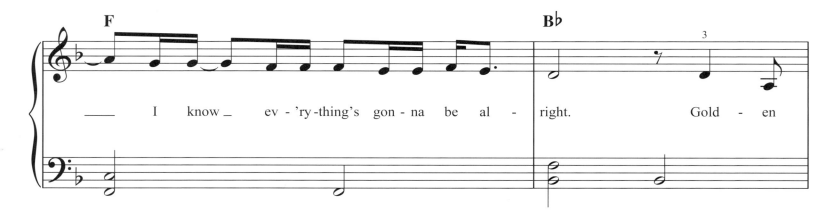

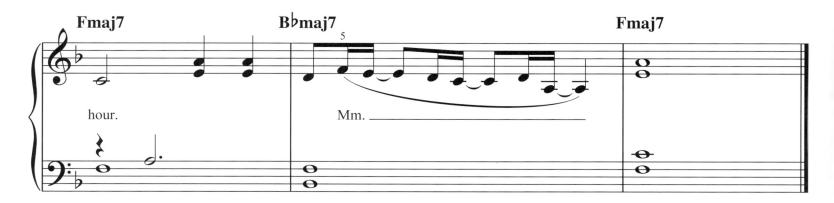

HIGH HORSE

Words and Music by KACEY MUSGRAVES,
TOMMY SCHLEITER and TRENT DABBS

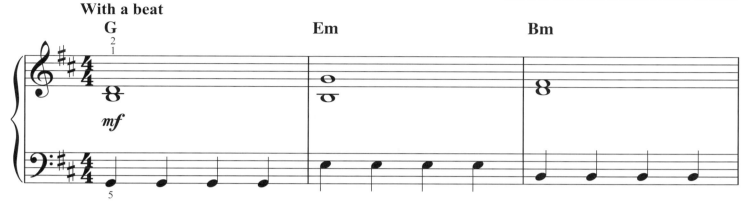

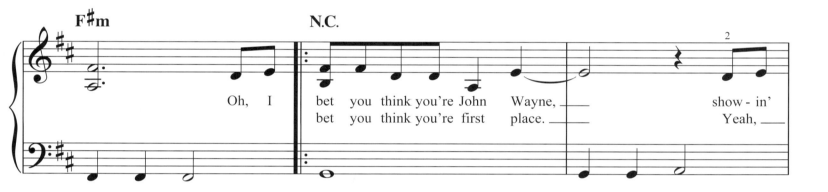

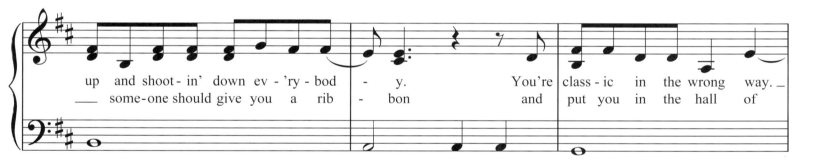

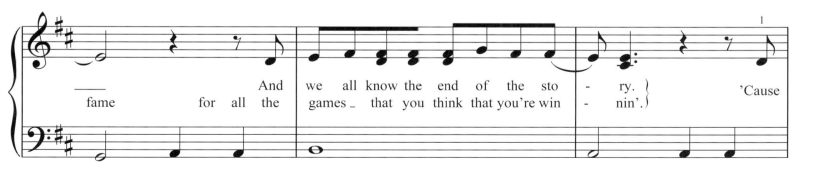

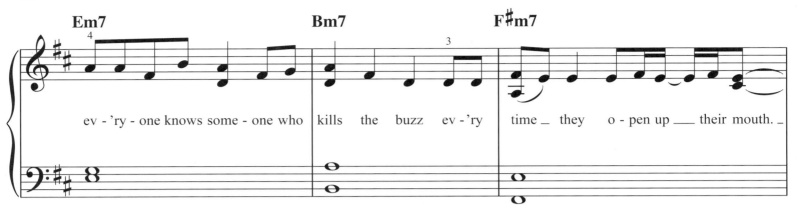

ev - 'ry - one knows some - one who kills the buzz ev - 'ry time __ they o - pen up __ their mouth. __

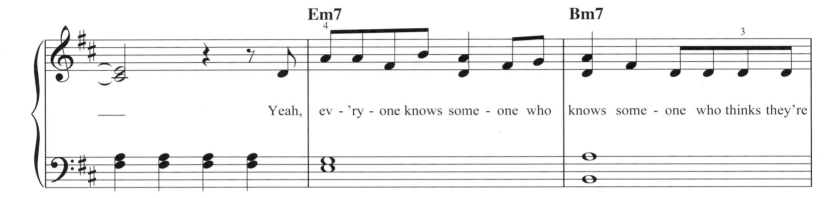

__ Yeah, ev - 'ry - one knows some - one who knows some - one who thinks they're

cool - er than ev - 'ry - bod - y else. __ And I think we've seen e - nough, seen e - nough __

to know that you ain't nev - er gon - na come down. __ So, why don't you

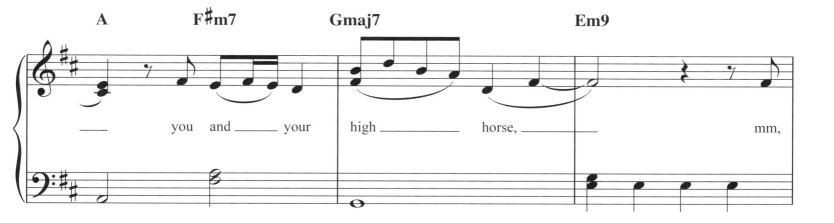

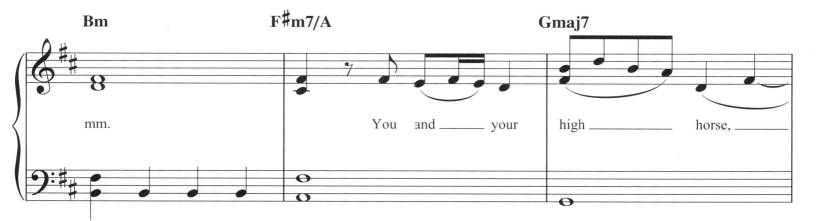

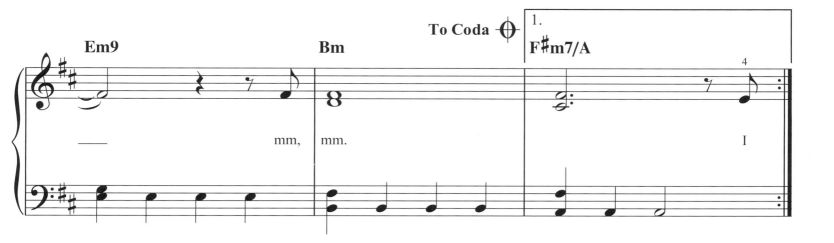

64

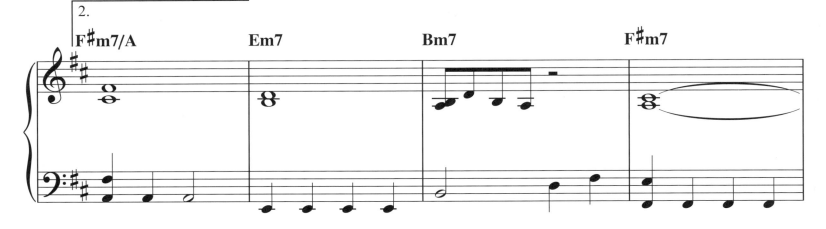

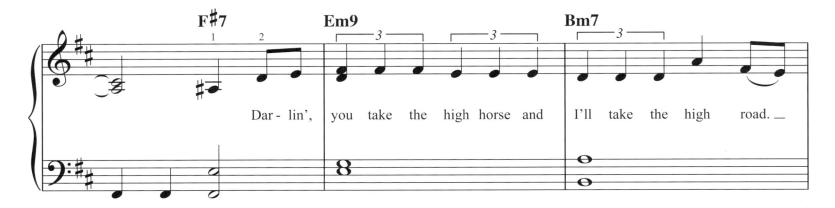

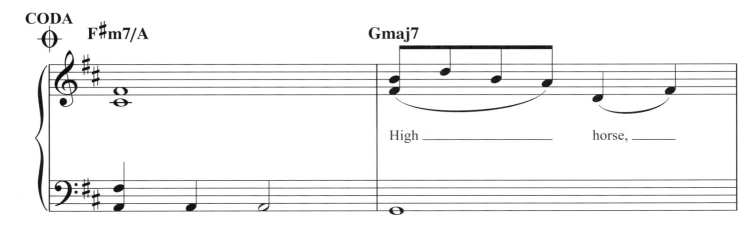

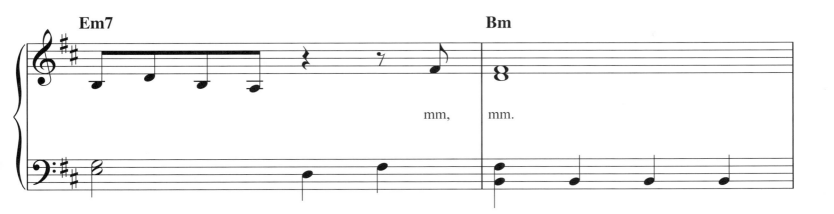

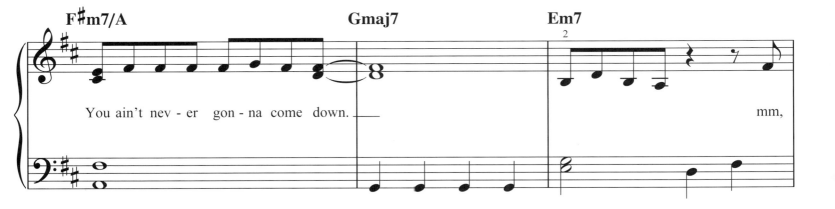

RAINBOW

Words and Music by KACEY MUSGRAVES,
SHANE McANALLY and NATALIE HEMBY

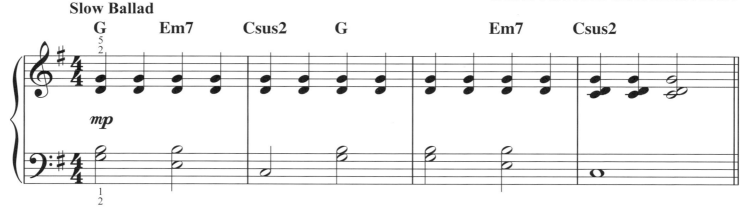

When it rains, __ it pours, __ but you did-n't e - ven no-tice it ain't

rain - ing an-y-more. __ It's hard to breathe when all __ you know is the

strug-gle of stay-ing __ a-bove __ the ris-ing wa-ter line. __

67

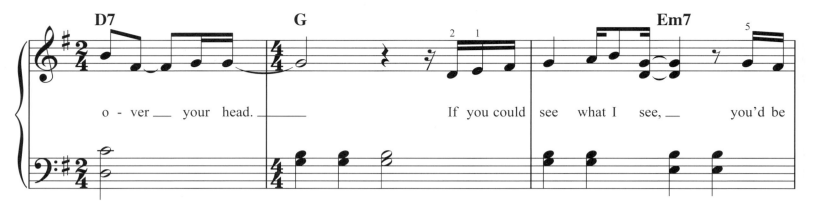

o - ver ___ your head. ___ If you could see what I see, ___ you'd be

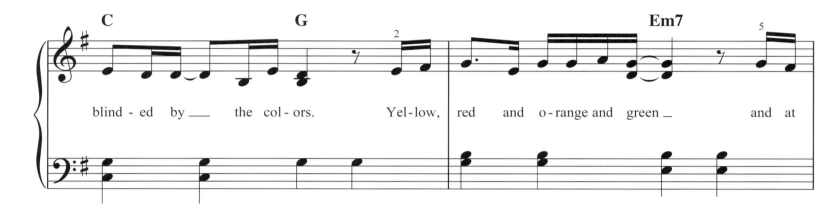

blind - ed by ___ the col - ors. Yel - low, red and o - range and green ___ and at

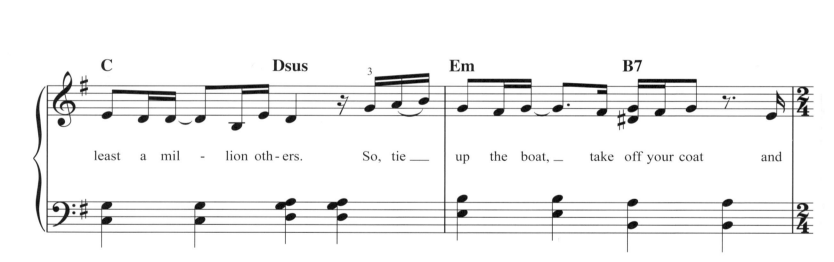

least a mil - lion oth - ers. So, tie ___ up the boat, ___ take off your coat and

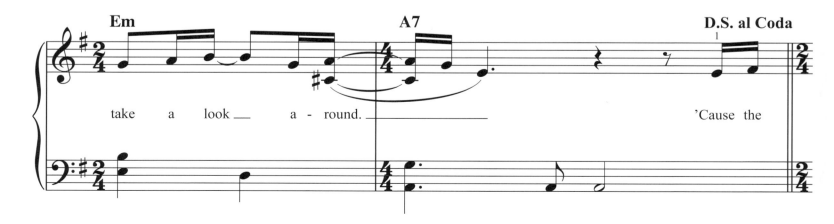

take a look ___ a - round. _____ 'Cause the

o - ver ____ your head. ____

Oh, tie up the boat, _ take off your coat ____ and

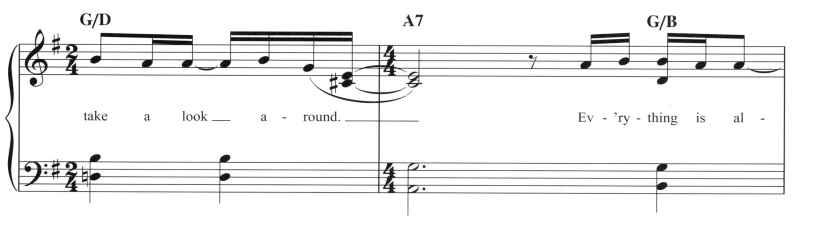

take a look ___ a - round. ____ Ev - 'ry - thing is al -

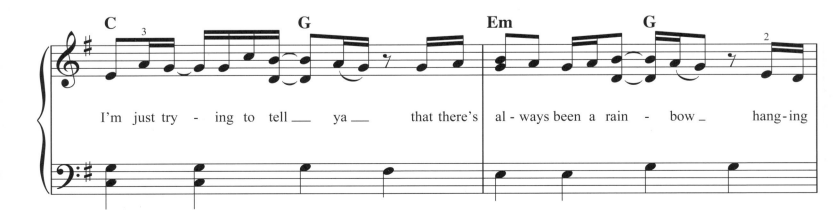

71

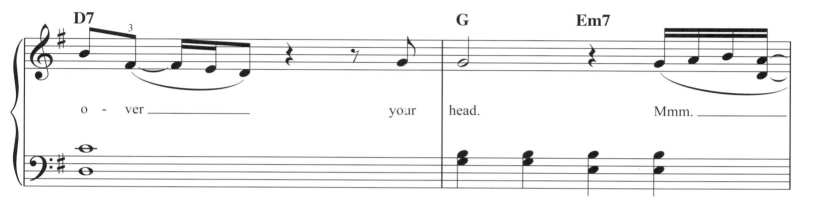

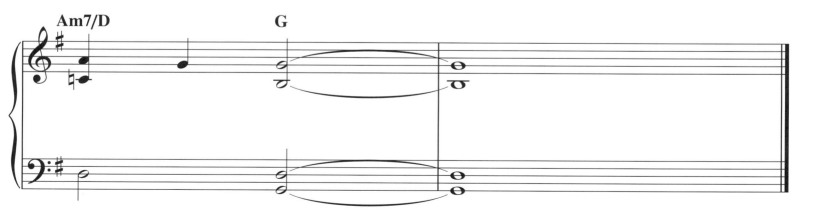